Anxiety

MANDI ROBBINS

ISBN 978-1-0980-5908-8 (paperback)
ISBN 978-1-0980-5909-5 (digital)

Christian Faith Publishing, Inc.
832 Park Avenue
Meadville, PA 16335
www.christianfaithpublishing.com

Printed in the United States of America

To God, who has poured out His love, grace, and mercy, my husband Kyle, and our son Kolbin.
I love you.

CONTENTS

INTRODUCTION

As a follower of Jesus, I always try to put Him first and let people see the Holy Spirit in me, working through me. I want people to look at me and know that my smile is filled with Jesus! I want people to feel better after they have talked with me. I want everyone I meet to see the light of Jesus, which is so hard at times when I am left with a debilitating condition called anxiety, but we can change the world for Jesus even with anxiety. *"And we know that for those who love God all things work together for good, for those who are called according to his purpose"* *(Romans 8:28)*.

God has chosen all of us to share his light and love on the hilltop. The devil will do all he can to block our path. Sometimes he is successful, but we must fight the good fight and continue the journey God has laid before us. We must always be wearing our armor, the full armor of God. *"Put on the whole armor of God, that you may be able to stand against the schemes of the devil"* (Ephesians 6:11).

It has taken a few years for this book to come to fruition but it is all in God's timing. I never imagined I would be diagnosed with general anxiety disorder and panic attacks but here I am, and I must press on and lean into God. My prayer is that someday I can put the anxiety and panic behind me. Life is too precious when every day is a gift from God. Let me take you on my journey.

Chapter 1

MY BEGINNINGS

I grew up in a broken family. My mom and biological father divorced when I was a toddler and he was out of the picture. I am forever grateful for God's intervention because I met the man I call "dad" who raised me and my siblings and still to this day I am very close to him. My mom and dad separated after thirteen years but I stayed with him. We farmed our whole lives and I wanted to stay and continue to help him; I am a daddy's girl and I love farming. When you grow up on a farm you grow up fast. No days off and work before play. I matured quickly and had a lot of responsibilities at a young age. We live in different states now, but I am thankful for the telephone and he is only a three-hour drive. I have a relationship with my mom who also lives out of state, but she tries to visit once-twice a year. Recently I have started a relationship with my biological father and it is going well. We have met for dinners, a few holidays, and talk on a regular basis. Our relationship is growing stronger and our son is excited when he sees grandpa. God works in amazing ways and through Him we can forgive and move forward. I am thankful for that. I have a brother, three sisters, a nephew, and seven nieces. I have been happily married for almost eleven years and we have an eight-year-old son. I love my family even though we have our times of difficulty. Who does not? I know my background has brought me lots of anxiety, trauma, and stress but I serve a big God who is helping me let go of the past.

My early church

I remember visiting many different churches growing up, we moved around often, different denominations, different states. The first church I attended was at the end of our dead-end road, I was probably around six or seven years old. I would ride my bike and attend many Sundays. I always felt something more was calling me to visit churches growing up. I now know that feeling was God. He had a plan for my life, even at a young age He was calling me. *"Before I formed you in the womb, I knew you" (Jeremiah 1:5).* I am His daughter.

Although I visited churches throughout my younger years, I did not learn much from it and do not really remember much about those Sundays. I felt that I went through the motions and church was fun because we sang, ate snacks, watched movies, played games, and heard a few Bible stories. I do not recall much honestly because I was only learning about God on Sundays. I did not remember much about God throughout the week, if anything at all. Being taught the Bible should not just happen at church, the most important place is at home. We should not hold the church accountable for raising our kids to know Christ. Our relationship with Him should not just happen on Sunday mornings. We need God every day. When we wake up, throughout the day, and when we lay our heads down at night. We simply did not have enough church at home. That is how it stayed until I met my husband.

He was in the military and went to church occasionally growing up. It was not until we moved back to his hometown where his Grandma would invite us to church every week. We slowly began attending, and the more we went, the more we learned about Jesus, our Savior, and the more our lives began to change. We were regularly attending in 2008 and were saved and baptized on July 25, 2009. Best day ever!

Who I am

I am your typical type A person. I am a non-stop, go getter, "let's finish what we started"—type of gal. I am a perfectionist and accept nothing less from myself. I like to control every situation and be organized. I plan months in advance. I usually have our son's birthday party planned out two to three months and VBS decorations for church ready four months before we need them. Our Christmas cards are sent out in October! I am strong-willed, stubborn, and won't back down easily. I have an incredibly competitive side when playing games, and that is why my friends nicknamed me, "the hammer." When I have a list of twenty tasks on a given day to accomplish, I will get thirty of them done. When I run my errands, I make sure that I can get every one of them done that day but nowadays my husband does all of them with me. I lay out a map in my head and we start in one direction and go in a circle and finish back at home. I like to be efficient.

I am more of a homebody now since anxiety and panic attacks have unwelcomed themselves in my life. I am an overthinker and I over analyze *everything*! Did I mention that I am a fighter? Not an octagon MMA fighter but one who must challenge everything. Doctors, lab work, my health, etc. My husband has his hands full.

I love to laugh, and smile and those days seem so few and far between now. Before anxiety settled in, I was an extrovert and loved hanging out with friends and making plans. Life is fuller when it is spent surrounded by others. I am also a giver. I love to help those in need. We are called to take care of others. *"She opens her hand to the poor and reaches out her hands to the needy" (Proverbs 31:20).* You can call me, and I'll help in any way I can even when I'm dealing with anxiety. I try to push the feelings away long enough to lend a helping hand, but sometimes the anxiety shows its ugly face. Most people do not know I struggle with anxiety, so I must play it off well. I like to stay busy in my church and community. This has been extremely hard to keep up with since anxiety and panic attacks have started. I have had to drop out of many things at church because of anxiety. Avoidance is not the best plan, but it works for me and it's what I feel is okay for now, and gives me momentary relief.

My husband often tells me my heart is too big because I end up carrying everyone else's burdens and it leads to more worry and stress. I'm a fixer, I want to help. I worry about my family, friends, strangers, the news, and the list goes on and on. I deleted Facebook for a while because it is sad, and upsetting, and doesn't help with my anxiety. I already have enough negativity. I now make sure to limit my time and unfollow anyone who posts negative things.

Unfortunately, I cannot keep going on like I have been. My mind and body consume this stress that result in uncontrollable anxiety outbursts. Anxiety is debilitating and sucks the life right out of you. As I write this book, I pray I can find comfort in sharing my story and pray that my story will impact and help others. My husband and our son are my biggest fans and I look forward to the day I feel normal again and can live the life God has set out for me and not the one Satan thinks I will keep.

Chapter 2

HERE TO STAY

Four years. Four years and counting, I have known the feelings and effects of anxiety and panic attacks. Honestly, it feels like forever when it is an everyday struggle. I know others who have dealt with this longer and I sometimes wonder how they keep pressing on? I feel death is at my door daily. I wish more than anything to go back and be able to change it with the snap of my fingers, but we all know it does not work that way. Some of you may be new to anxiety and some of you may be a veteran. Either way, I pray for all who deal with this devil. So many people suffer from anxiety and I really prefer not to talk about mine because it simply makes me anxious.

According to "Anxiety and Depression Association Of America" (2010–2018), "Anxiety disorders are the most common mental illness in the US, affecting forty million adults in the United

States age eighteen and older, or 18.1% of the population every year." Forty million adults just in the United States! That is a big number. I know society places a stigma on mental health but do not worry. It is what it is. I am not ashamed of my anxiety anymore. I do not care if I've been labeled. You should not be ashamed either. We never asked for this and we are trying our best to fight it and beat it. This world is harsh and if someone makes fun of you for it or does not think it's a big deal, pray for them and move on. Turn the other cheek. No need to argue with them, we do that enough with ourselves, just smile and stroll on.

So why do so many suffer? A possibility would be that life flies by so fast because we as a society are way too busy. "We" want the next best thing, the car, house, vacation, clothes, more money, work, and the list can go on and on, but all this causes stress. We are always in a hurry and I definitely fit in this category! It scares me to be quiet and still. I feel purpose when I have something to do or a million things to do. God didn't create us for hurry. He knew we would need rest and He gave that to us, but it's up to us to take the gift. We beat ourselves up going one hundred mph and really for what? Are we satisfied, truly satisfied with the fast lifestyle? We spend our entire lives searching, but all we need is Jesus. He can fill your void.

What can we do to change this? We need to find rest in our Lord, our Father. We need to slow down and really look at what is important and what can wait. We allow all the baggage to consume us and then we get stuck. In our own way, we try to unpack it and end up with the same stress we were trying to shake. Our bodies and minds were not built to handle this in our own way. We need to reevaluate who God intended us to be. If we do not do anything about it, the numbers will stay the same or rise. Only a small percentage seeks help. While there are many ways to deal with anxiety, it is easier when Jesus is by your side. I cannot even fathom what my life would be like without Jesus going through this part with me. Being one of these statistics, God has led me to write this book and when he calls, be obedient. He will use this how He sees fit. Thy will be done, right? We are always to be a servant to God even during our trials and tribulations.

Sometimes I feel like Job. I pray God never allows Satan to test me that far, but my heart aches for what Job went through during his struggles. *"So I am allotted months of emptiness, and nights of misery are apportioned to me. When I lie down I say, "When shall I arise?" But the night is long, and I am full of tossing till the dawn"* (Job 7:3–4). So many nights I felt and still feel like Job. We all have struggles and they are all different, but we serve the same God who can get us through them. Job's misery was temporary and if you have read the book of Job then you know the ending was amazing. *"And the Lord blessed the latter days of Job more than his beginning"* (Job 42:12). If you haven't read the book of Job, please do! God was with him the whole time, as He is with us. I know the truth in that previous statement can *feel* so false at times. We search and search the Lord and yet feel empty sometimes. He has not turned away from us, He is there. There is nothing that you or I have done that would ever make God turn from us. I am sure you are ready to be done naming and claiming anxiety just as much as I am. Anxiety has consumed me, and I want my life back.

Chapter 3

THE DOWNFALL

May 2016, I was awakened by an unsettling feeling. I fell asleep snuggling with our son but wasn't asleep long before I began to feel nauseous and dizzy. I walked out to the kitchen to see my husband and told him that I wasn't feeling well. He hugged me and then got me a glass of water. Up to this point my family has been blessed with good health, praise *God*! My husband has only had the stomach bug once since we have been together and that's over thirteen years now. Our son has only been sick three times since birth and up until this evening I hadn't been sick in a few years. I paced back and forth in the bathroom as I was just uneasy, and eventually I settled back into bed thinking I will be sick tomorrow. All I could think of was I don't have time to be sick! I don't like being sick. Not that anyone does. Yeah, I was sick but not necessarily physically.

Over the course of the next two weeks I would get this same unsettling feeling and I would get light-headed, dizzy, and nauseous. I have never experienced this before, so I was becoming quite worried. I am a worrywart, and this was not helping. These symptoms would show up no matter what time of day or night. I was starting to be afraid to leave our home. I was also fearful of passing out while driving with our son. Something was not right.

I only see my doctor for yearly exams if that. Not the place I prefer to spend my time. I made an appointment to see my doctor. My doctor wanted to get some blood work, conduct an exam, and go over some questions. My plan was to get diagnosed and have a prescription to make me better. Well, she checked me out all right, she decided to give me aspirin and place an oxygen mask on me! She said she was not worried but wanted to send me to the ER for more testing. I did not care if she wasn't worried as this was happening to me and I was scared, sad, mad, upset, and worried. I walked into her office but went out in a wheelchair!

Once I arrived at the ER, they rushed me to a room and hooked an EKG up. The nurse drew blood and I waited. Finally, after a few hours, the doctor came in and told me my labs and EKG were normal and he sent me home. I was left wondering, what just happened? Apparently, I am not alright because I am having recurring symptoms of light-headedness and nauseous feelings. Pregnancy was out of the question and I did not have other symptoms at that time. On the other hand, I was thanking God that everything they tested me for came back normal. I asked to be placed on the prayer chain at church while I was at the ER. It is imperative to have prayer warriors! I was still afraid there was something medically wrong with me and God was getting ready for me.

The weekend rolled around, and our son was staying with his Pappy and Mimi so that my husband and I could enjoy a date day. We know how hard it can be to plan a date after you become a parent. It feels like an eternity sometimes. So, we headed to a mall about an hour from home. We went shopping, ate lunch, and were headed to the last stop before going back to pick up our son. I remember my husband turning the car off and he was about to open his door when all of a sudden, *bam*, I started to feel light-headed and weird again. I told him how I was feeling, he asked me a few questions and said we could just go home. That sounded like a perfect plan except now my heart was starting to race, my breathing increased. I felt like I was hyperventilating, my left arm was starting to feel numb, and my body was tingling and beginning to shake. In a loud voice I said, "Please call the ambulance." Okay, I was screaming in fear! I did not know what was happening to me! "Get me to a hospital!" Neither of us knew where the nearest hospital was since we were in unfamiliar territory. Of course, the moment you need it, the blue sign with the letter H on it is nowhere in sight. Ugh, I felt like I was going to die that day at age thirty. My husband drove down the road while on the phone with 911 then he pulled into a parking lot and we waited for help. I still felt like I couldn't breathe and now my whole body was shaking, and I was crying. I don't know how long it took the ambulance, but it sure felt like forever. I felt stiff even though I had all these actions happening to my body.

The EMTs arrived and asked me a few questions. They gave me an aspirin and told me I would be headed to the hospital. Meanwhile my husband was dialing our family pastor and asking for continued prayers. I thought I was literally dying! As they were loading me in the ambulance, I was praying I would be alright. This was my first ambulance ride, which added more stress and anxiety. My husband had to follow us in the car, and I hated that he couldn't be with me in the ambulance. The EMT was talking with me and checking something behind my head often. I assume my heart rate, but I don't remember being hooked up to anything. Many things can become blurry when you are in that state of mind. He told me he thought I was having a panic attack. A what? I never heard of such a thing. He did not elaborate, so that was no help to someone who was clearly in need of an explanation. Thankfully, the ride was not too long. I was pulled from the ambulance and wheeled into the ER. I kept my eyes shut as they quickly moved me to a room because I felt everyone was watching me. They ran a series of tests and after some time had passed, the doctor concluded that I did in fact have a panic attack. Again, what? How did this happen? Why did this happen? How do I get rid of it? Are they sure that is what it was? Will it happen again? Are these symptoms related to the other symptoms I have had the last few weeks? Why? Why? Why? All the questions flooded my mind and I certainly did not want it to happen again. If you have ever experienced a panic attack you know exactly how I felt! They really did not answer anything other than my symptoms showed a panic attack and it can happen when you're stressed. He gave me some medicine to calm me down and it helped. The ER doctor told me to follow up with my family doctor and said I could go home. By this time, I was so exhausted, I just wanted to sleep. It felt like my body ran a marathon without my consent, and I am not a runner.

Monday came and I needed to drop off the ER paperwork to my doctor's office. While in the waiting room, guess what happened? Yes, another panic attack. The attack this time was not as extreme, but nonetheless an attack. I was at the secretary's desk when I started to feel light-headed. I told the secretary how I was feeling and asked if they had an open room. I prefer that no one sees me in this state, and I had no idea what might happen this time. Thankfully, they had an open room and they let me sit there while they got my doctor. The doctor checked me over and looked at the paperwork from the weekend ER visit, then asked me if I felt stressed? I wanted to laugh because I am always stressed. Who isn't? What's life without stress?

I told my doctor we recently moved my sister and her two kids in with us. We were trying to help my sister recover from prescription drug addiction. She had been a drug addict for years. She is a single mother that refused to go back to rehab, so she was detoxing in our home. She did not want to lose her kids and we were her last hope at help. The devil was surely raging war in my house. Add that to me being a stay-at-home mom who takes care of our son, daily house chores, meals, homework, family time, and in the beginning stages of starting a non-profit to help homeless families. Stress was written across my whole body in bright ink! My world was crashing, and I felt like it was crashing fast. So yeah, I am stressed! After hearing all that, the doctor prescribed me medication that hopefully would help with the panic attacks. I was willing to try it because I obviously could not get through a full day without a panic attack or feeling disconnected.

I had to hide the medication from my recovering sister. Thanks, Doc, for adding more stress. I am already stressed to the max and now I have to worry about my sister finding and abusing the medication. What were they giving me? I have never been one to take a lot of medication, over-the-counter or prescription. Although the panic attacks and anxiety came out with the added stress of my sister living with us, I do not blame my sister at all. It would have happened eventually. My body was a ticking time bomb. An explosion waiting to happen. My husband has told me for years that I worry too much, I stress too much, and he was right. It finally caught up to me. Thirty years of trying to handle everything on my own when I should have been letting God handle it for me. I used to think I had to be strong and that I could handle it all. I had prayed many years off and on to have the opportunity to help my sister beat this addiction. God answered my prayer for her, but His mission was not just about my sister, it included me too.

My sister is doing amazing to this day. She is still in recovery, has been saved, baptized, and is living her life for Jesus. I was thankful for that opportunity to serve God and help my sister. I wish this was the end of my story and that the medicine worked and la de da, but not even close.

Chapter 4
SYMPTOMS

I started to have multiple panic attacks every day and found it hard to function at all. Within a month or so, I had seen a handful of different doctors from the same office, prescribed a variety of different medications (none of which helped), been to the ER at least five more times, and now experiencing additional symptoms. I am a tiny thing to begin with and I had lost ten pounds in a week due to severe stomach pains and not being able to eat. I felt like my skin was on fire. I was crying all day uncontrollably, my left shoulder hurt. I wanted to just lie in bed, I was at the end of my rope. When leaving the house people would comment on how bony and sick I looked. Yes, thank you, like I did not notice. I was not trying to lose any weight, it just left. I did not want to leave my house anymore.

Trying to do everything for the household and follow Christ while suffering with anxiety was making me miserable. Why was God allowing me this much pain? Why was He not giving me comfort during this time? If not physically then mentally. I really felt no hope, and this was going to be my new life. There is a reason for this season, right? Out of all those visits, my diagnosis came down to severe panic attacks and general anxiety disorder. It started with the day I had the first panic attack. I relentlessly kept telling myself something else was wrong with me. Remember, I am a fighter.

Nothing the doctors prescribed or advised was giving me any relief. During another appointment, my doctor said I needed to get more help. I could not agree more! I had been praying through all of this, yet God did not feel near. Where was He? I realize now that I was placing my situation above God and struggling to give control to God. I had been through so much in such a short amount of time. Who is this person I have become? After another ER visit, my doctor thought it would be best for me to be admitted to the psychiatric ward at a different hospital. I would try anything at this point, so I agreed. I could not continue to live in the state I was in. I was not happy about leaving my son and husband for three days. I wanted to get better, so I went. I did not realize that you were not allowed to have anything in there. I had to ask for my toothbrush! It was serious business in there and it scared me. Everyone is in there for different reasons. I understand why they use precaution and do what they do. That just put me on edge. All I was allowed was my Bible and another book.

During my three-day stay, I attended all the meetings and appointments with the doctors there. They wanted to place me on a new medicine that would help me sleep and help ease my anxiety. The doctors consulted my husband and we all agreed to try it. Worst case would be an allergic reaction that could lead to hospitalization, but I was already hospitalized. What do I have to lose? I felt like I lost just about everything including my mind, so let us give this a try.

The nurse brought me my first pill and I remember playing cards with a few other patients, but the one lady I was playing cards with warned me when I stood up, I may have a woozy feeling. She was on that same medicine before. About twenty minutes later, I felt tired and got up, and yes, I had to hold on to the railing to get to my room. I was not so sure about this pill and that made me more anxious. Well, I slept fairly good for a while then my light was turned on and I saw people in my room with another patient. I was so tired and drowsy I just hoped I would be okay with a roommate. I just wanted to be by myself and quiet. Morning came and the doctors were surrounding my bed. They had to wake me up because it was time for breakfast and meetings. I guess I did get some sleep! I was very tired throughout the day though. To this point I have been having two panic attacks a day, one in the morning and one in the evening for days but this was a new day, a different day. The morning after that first dose I did not have a single panic attack! What? I even started to eat again after losing all the weight to my stomach hurting. I felt like this was going to work. The downside of this medicine is that I felt tired and not myself. It was like I had tunnel vision, simply weird and blah. Although, who are we kidding, I have not been myself for some time now! I mentioned feeling tired and sluggish to the nurse and she suggested taking the pill earlier and then going straight to bed. I followed her advice and I continued to feel tired. My wonderful husband came every night to check on me during visiting hours. It surely helped to see his face. Finally, the third day arrived, and he came to take me home. I could not wait to run out of there. I missed our son and thought I would be better.

During that short stay, I was able to talk about God to a few of the patients. During our group discussion time I said I was thankful for this experience because God would use it how he needed to. Sometimes I want to question that last statement of being thankful for that experience because I am still struggling. He was using it to help me and those I encountered including my roommate. This was not her first time in the ward, and she was suicidal. The first thing she told me she noticed was my Bible on my nightstand. I just started a conversation with her and those few days we were able to talk a lot about our faith. She has a beautiful family and is a believer. She had been struggling for years but still had faith. God knew we would be together, and he used me to help her. *"For I know the plans I have for you, declares the Lord, plans for welfare and not for evil, to give you a future and a hope" (Jeremiah 29:11).* I thought leaving those doors behind me was a new beginning and, in a way, it was, but it just didn't last.

Once home, I continued the medicine and checked in with the doctors from the hospital. The medicine did help me sleep, and it also made me want to eat and I gained my ten pounds back in a week! But all day, every day, for the few weeks I stayed on it I was tired, sluggish, felt lazy, didn't want to get out of bed, and exhausted. The only positive was being able to eat and sleep again. I cannot continue to feel and function this way with the busy household I have. There had to be another option. I was prescribed the lowest dose and the doctors said that if I cut the pill in half it would be stronger. I cannot figure that out and don't care to. I stopped taking the medicine after seeking professional advice in hopes my body calmed down enough that I would be normal again. This is where the anxiety kicked up a few notches. Did I make the right choice? Did the cons outweigh the pros? Did the pros outweigh the cons? Were they sure it's anxiety? I was convinced my symptoms were physical not mental. The physical pains were still wearing me down every second of the day and the stomach pains had returned, this time more severe, leading to more ER visits. I now feel like a regular when before I would stay away from a hospital at all costs. I have been there so often that I felt they were not helping me, they would look at my chart, throw a pill my way, and say take this, relax, and you can go home. Yeah, thanks because that will solve my problem. I would refuse to take it because they were just masking the problem and I wanted answers! Why is my body continuing to do this? Why do I feel like this? Do I have to take medication that numbs me to everything, so I do not have an attack? Will this be the new and forever me as we know it? God, where are you? I am praying, my church is praying, my friends, my family, I am covered in prayer, yet I am still struggling with this. I know all who suffer are not always healed. God hears every one of their prayers for me and He is there. Trusting in Him no matter what we are going through or not going through is key. That is faith. God knows my whole story, I do not. God is our great physician and I know He can heal me mentally and physically at any time. I know I can still lean on Him and continue to pray that this too shall pass. Through this journey I keep telling myself that there is always hope in Jesus.

Some more time had passed, and I had been seen by more doctors, specialists, ER visits, and lost the ten pounds I gained back. I cannot even tell you how many appointments I had in a week, too many. Finally, I was admitted to the hospital for my stomach pain and had some procedures done the next day. To my dismay everything came back normal. Normal? What is that? Obviously, they missed something again! I still have no energy, chronic stomach pains, cannot eat and I just want to put this all behind me and never look back. You will not have to worry about me turning into a pillar of salt because I am running away from it! (See Genesis 19.) Realizing now I was trying to run from it but not running one hundred percent to God. My anxiety and panic are trying to be bigger than God and that just cannot be! I praised God time and time again for all the tests coming back normal but I am still struggling with anxiety and panic attacks. Was this in my head? Am I that messed up? Have the doctors been right the whole time? What is going on? Lord, please help me! I need to feel your presence. Who am I? Who have I become?

Shortly after my stomach pains left, another symptom showed up. Now I am starting to have chest pains. I could have any pain in my body, why in my chest? Now tell me you would not freak out. Doctors seem to see my symptoms all the same, I felt like I was not being taken seriously. I wore a heart monitor for twenty-four hours and that checked out fine. Praise the Lord! I had nine electrocardiographs done on my heart with all my hospital visits and they were all normal. I cannot even count how many blood tests and other procedures I went through. What is happening? I am feeling all these pains and they are real and crippling! Something must be wrong with my heart because these pains are different from my previous chest pains. I'm afraid to exercise now because my heart will beat fast, which it should when you're getting a great workout in, but I had a panic attack once when I was exercising and now my mind associates exercise with panic and I'm currently not exercising like I should be. God, seriously! Why? Why do I suffer? How are you using this pain for good? This broken sinful world really stinks!

I noticed after some time that I was getting gassy during the chest pains and if I would have entered a burping contest, I would have won hands down. Probably still could. This pain hurt so much that it felt like a heart attack and there I am on my knees praying one night after dinner in our bedroom, please do not let me die. Thankfully that pain eventually subsided. The pain however would return and lead to another doctor visit. I am now being diagnosed with silent acid reflux known as GERD. How did I go from a healthy thirty-year-old who never goes to the doctor to this person I am now in a matter of months? Another diagnosis, another medicine to try for another symptom that just popped up. Well I tried the medicine off and on for several months and did not feel much relief.

I decided that I would research what I could do about GERD. They say your stomach is your second brain. I have read articles claiming you're eating habits and anxiety can go hand in hand. Please do not assume everything we read is true and/or false. I prefer the natural route over medicinal after what I had been through, but I was willing to try anything to get rid of that pain. So, I stopped eating dairy and went gluten free. I probably should have chosen to do one first then the other, but I was desperate to cut out whatever might be causing that pain, if it was even from that. That is the anxiety talking. Always arguing with myself. One part of our brain talks us into things while the other part argues with it. The several months that I was dairy- and gluten-free I did find some relief and noticed I was not as gassy, and the pain was bearable but still scary. I am still here so I tell myself it must be my GERD or anxiety. My luck it is both. I am not telling you to go off any medication and do not just follow what I did. You should always check with a medical professional. I am not a professional, just a struggler. Anxiety can cause our bodies to do some pretty messed up things. GERD was just another diagnosis added to my list.

I worry about everything I put in my body. I read all the labels before I eat something. Will this cause me heartburn, reflux, or something else? I try to buy organic and purchase items with the least amount of preservatives. Grocery shopping is hard nowadays. It takes me longer in a grocery store than it used to and I worry about food served at parties and get-togethers, because of that, I try to avoid social events. I have real concerns about what we put into our bodies. Sometimes I have to just ask my husband to get groceries, so I don't have to deal with it.

My efforts were not completely successful, leading to more visits to the doctor for chest pain and now I am scheduled for a stress test. Great, here we go again. Thankfully, that came back normal and the medical technician said I have a textbook heart, which is a great thing! My anxious mind had to know the results. I figured the chest pain would eventually subside like my stomach pains, but it did not. I had that chest pain every day for a year! A *year*! I concluded that it must be my mind tricking me again. Right? Is it? My tests still show a healthy person. Does anxiety really have that much power?

Yes, it does! I will add that I was panic attack-free for almost a year. Thankfully for a while I had them under control and fought hard when they tried to creep up. Panic attacks can just happen whether you are stressed or feel calm. Panic attacks happen a lot more when you are dealing with high anxiety. Why do I have new symptoms every now and again? How is it possible for my body and mind to do things I would rather it not? How do my nerves cause all these random pains and ailments at the same time or different times? Why can't I live the life I had years ago? I bet you have had these questions and probably more. I am with you. Believe me I have been there, am still there, but I do not plan on staying. I pray you do not either. God created us for more.

Chapter 5

ADDITIONAL HELP

More time passed and I still struggled with physical ailments and anxiety. My husband suggested that I talk with a therapist again. We never argued about it, I just talked myself out of it and smiled at him. I tried a psychologist after my first few panic attacks, and it didn't work out. I was just uncomfortable and wanted to be secluded. I prefer not to see one because that meant I would have to make time, find a babysitter, drive by myself, talk about my anxiety, and I felt I could be doing other things on my agenda. I would rather talk to my husband or my best friend of thirty years. When you have anxiety you usually have what we call, a safe person. My husband and my best friend are my safe people. Yes, I have two! They help calm me down and talk me through things. I understand his concern because his wife has been "missing" for a few years. He wants to see me happy and healthy again and feels seeing someone can help. We have an amazing marriage and always have but I am afraid of everything on a much higher scale than before. I worry about everything times one thousand or more. These physical and mental symptoms are too much to handle day in and day out. My husband loved me then, now, and will. In sickness and in health, until death do us part. God knew exactly what He was doing when He placed us together. My husband just wants the best for me, to be healthy, mentally and physically.

I decided to give the counseling thing another try, but I wanted to see a therapist that believed in Jesus. Although if a Christian counselor was not an option, I would take the opportunity given by God to disciple to a therapist that was not a Christian. Would that be reverse psychology?

I wanted to conquer this through prayer and a Bible. I was not thinking about how God wanted to help me through this, but how I wanted to do this with God. "I" does not work without allowing God to help in His way. I thought I was following God's path, but, it has always been my way. During that time, I was still seeking, praying, and feeling what I was doing was the right thing. I was recommended to a Christian therapist by our lead pastor. I met with her off and on a handful of times for a few months. She recommended reading a book, working through a panic attack workbook, and trying belly breathing (which hurts and is uncomfortable for me), writing down my worries, which I did not do, mainly because I joked I would have a five subject notebook full by the time I saw her again. If you are reading this book, then you know that to be true. I don't prefer to see how crazy my mind truly is by writing it *all* down in *ink*! Anxiety fills our minds twenty-four seven and with scary stuff. Negative thoughts creep into every part of our life, all the time. I felt like I was just checking off another thing I had tried that was not working. Hard to break that habit. The counseling was short-lived because she was a twenty-minute drive near the city, didn't have evening hours, my husband can't continue to take off work, and I couldn't bring our son in with me to hear the things we needed to chat about. I have already noticed he is taking up some of my anxiety. I only trust a select few people to watch our son. Yes, the anxiety is high, can you tell? Majority of the selected few I trust work during the day, and I feel bad asking for help. Again, trying to do it on my own terms. My way.

I was seen by a psychiatrist too. I know they are not counselors but another thing I felt I had to do and see what he thought and what he would prescribe. That was a two-hour appointment and I was supposed to have a follow up but never did because I was afraid to take the medicine he prescribed. Another appointment cancelled and just another regular day in my life. There are so many medications and each professional wanted me to try a different one. No, thank you. I am not your guinea pig! Can't we get on the same page?

Since I have exhausted all the allopathic methods, now it is on to the holistic approach. I am terrified of pharmaceutical drugs and have not tried this avenue yet. I met with a wonderful holistic doctor, who was very friendly and awfully expensive. She also prayed with me at the end of our appointment, which made me feel better. She gave me some supplements to try. I started taking them but then like always, I freaked out and later that week they ended up in the trash. I really wanted this to be my last stop. I still could not grasp how I was physically and mentally healthy for so long and now this. Your life truly can change in the blink of an eye.

I have tried essential oils as well. I love my oils but again they are not strong enough for what I am dealing with. My cabinet is full of oils and they are my go-to for everything from our first aid kit, diffusing, recipes, and all-around serenity. I used the anxiety blend, massage oil, lavender, etc. you name it, I tried it. Again, they are helpful but not strong enough for my anxiety. I am not endorsing or recommending any oils or brands, but I continue to use them daily. I love my oils!

Nothing was working, so I decided to find a new doctor. I felt I got nowhere with my last doctor even though I had what they call the "million-dollar work up." Anxiety much? I wanted to talk with my new doctor about trying CBD oil. I have read a lot about its effect on anxiety over the last few years. Why not? I met with my new doctor and we discussed using CBD oil. My doctor supported what I had read and did not see any issue with me trying it. I thought it was great that he was on my page. I spent hours on the web and bought the best of the best, organic, all-natural CBD oil. I was ready to try it and I did. Nothing! I did not feel a difference at all. What! I have read all this great stuff on it. I met with my doctor again and he said everybody is different. I decided to try a different company and a different kind. The first one was a tincture and this second one was a spray you put in your drink.

It was bitter and gross but if it helped, I did not care how it tasted. Plug my nose and go. Well again nothing. What, how is this possible? Am I the only one this does not work for? The Internet and these companies make it sound so perfect.

Sometime later we had a store open in our area. My husband wanted to go the first day it opened but I was quite hesitant. We would drive by the store for months before I decided to try it again. One evening, we went in and talked with the owner and he was immensely helpful. I told him my previous failures with the oil, and he helped me understand the dosing. I had a tincture and water-soluble oil in hand to try before we left. The store owner gave me a sample while we were there, I took the sample but felt very anxious. I would love to say it helped and that is how I solved my anxiety issues, but it did not. I felt a little more at ease and I would love to take CBD on a regular basis just for the benefits but I unfortunately did not have the time to wait and increase my dose every few days to see what worked. I wanted something right then! I was still anxious as usual and experiencing panic attacks again. Please seek professional medical advice from your doctor before trying CBD.

Chapter 6

NEVER ENDING

I started having panic attacks out of the blue again and I try to do my best to ignore the symptoms. I pray, take deep breaths, and it helps when my husband is around to hold me and pray with me. I feel like there is a new symptom showing up once I get one under control. You know what I mean? In the last several months I have also experienced heart palpitations while trying to relax, and many mornings I wake up feeling my heart and chest beating a million miles per minute but when I check my heart rate, it is normal? What is that about? That can leave yesterday!

I feel as though I cannot get enough oxygen. I suffer daily trying to breathe normal but constantly feel the need to take deep breaths. I dislike new symptoms like one of the ten plagues! (See Exodus 7–11.) I dislike all the symptoms I have ever had but the reality is, did I think I would get through life without problems? Seriously, we live in a broken world, but we have hope in Jesus. It will not always be like this!

Jesus said I was worth it and so are you! If you feel alone, do not, because although I felt alone when praying during these times, He is there, He will always be there. I felt alone because nothing was changing for the better. Although it can be so hard to feel His presence, *He is there*! Allow God to be bigger than your worries, fears, and anxiety. "Don't dig up in doubt what you planted in faith" (Elisabeth Elliot). Our minds are powerful. Satan will use it to his advantage every chance he gets.

Another anxious day and I decided to take our son for a walk around town. As we were walking, I was silently crying and praying. I had tears running down my face, so I figured walking toward our church was a good place to go. I needed a tissue but when I entered, our friend and secretary was in the office. I asked her for tissues and then just broke down telling her I was having a panic attack. I tried to fight it but it is unbearable many times and hard to hide the attacks. She prayed with me and took our son for a bit so I could go calm down and pray in the sanctuary. I lay down in the pew praying, crying, and singing in my head. I was just begging God again to lift this from me. I ended up getting worse and thankfully my doctor's office was just a few blocks away and that is where I ended up.

As I was in the waiting room, so many thoughts entered my mind. Is there something wrong with me this time? Is it anxiety? Could I have saved myself from living this struggle by taking all the medicine and dealing with the other effects? Would the medicine have lasted and helped? Should I have just pushed through all the physical and mental side effects and feelings that the medicine was doing to me?

I decided to call my husband while waiting at the doctor's office and told him we needed to get away for the weekend and he agreed. We took a trip to visit my best friend's family out of state. We had a good weekend. The kids played, we crocheted. It was great as always. While visiting we attended her church, but I did not know at the time that there was a guest speaker that day. God knew I would be there; He knew what I needed. He always knows what we need before we do. At the end of the sermon there was an altar call for healing. Go figure. He knows! I knew I needed physical healing for sure. If God would heal me physically then I would be fine mentally. The physical pains cause me more anxiety. Throughout the whole message I had tight chest pains. I did not want to go up in front of the congregation because I am strong, remember. I didn't want to look weak in my faith, but in reality, it takes great strength to admit you need help. I am also prideful. I knew I had faith! I knew I would cry…a lot. I would have been okay waiting to talk with the speaker and being prayed over after church, but my best friend had her arm wrapped around my right arm and my husband's arm was wrapped around my left. She asked me to go up and be prayed over and I felt my husband let go and she pulled me toward the front. We are both bawling by now and she wanted the speaker to specifically pray over me. Now the whole congregation is behind me and I have no tissues. I am exhausted from all this anxiety and the pain my body has been through. I believe in healing. Why have I not received it? Or have I and I've been just somehow subconsciously denying it? I am blessed and thankful for life everyday but is God going to allow me to live this way the rest of my life? Why am I not feeling better? Why is this not past me? Why is it that I am still dealing with this? I wanted God to help me, I wanted to be healed of all this baggage, all the pain, all the symptoms, everything. I wanted to be healed naturally not medicinally. Medicine is important, I understand, God helps through medicine. I just wanted God to give me a miracle. Instant healing at an altar call! This is what I wanted! As I was being prayed for, I felt the chest pain leave, amen. I could not speak but just cry, tell God I am sorry and please heal me and help me move on from this chapter of my life. He has big plans for my life and is not ready for me yet. I was prayed over by the speaker's husband as well and he prayed things never mentioned before that only my best friend and husband would know. We were amazed! God is amazing! I felt relief and happiness. I stood there with my best friend and husband while we sang and rocked back and forth. I wanted God to take the pains and anxiety and keep it! For real! God can certainly heal us instantly but that is not always His will for our lives. He is our great physician. He sees the bigger picture; He knows us fully.

I did not receive a miracle that day, but that is okay. It is not in God's plan and I am okay with that. I must be. Miracles still happen, believe that! The Holy Spirit was with me and for a brief moment I felt calmed on the inside and relaxed knowing God had me. God was showing me that He is here for me. He hears me. He loves me.

Chapter 7

DIVINE SUPPORT

You have heard the saying, "God won't give you more than you can handle." Well, He does because we need Him every day. Our eyes should be on Him the whole time. If He did not give us more than what we could handle we would not need Him. *We need Him*! I am not saying we do not have the ability to handle certain situations because God has equipped us in amazing ways to deal with this broken life but mentally it is too much, at least for me.

Some days I get in a good Bible study and other days I do not. The reason for this is that my mind is filled with other things I feel I must do. It is about choice. God gave us freedom. Be careful how you use it. He deserves me first and I need Him first before life happens. I feel my best when I start with His word in the morning. My days are brighter, I have more patience, happier, and the list goes on.

That is all hard to keep when anxiety tries to creep in before lunch or even before I get out of bed. I need to find peace. Peace through God and not the peace from getting my lists completed and feeling accomplished. Reality is, that does not bring true peace. It brings more chaos. Only God can give us true peace. I have yearned for the peace I hear many talk about. How do I get there? How do you get there? What does it really mean to be at peace with God?

I have realized that I have always been afraid of many things my whole life. My husband tells me that I have had decades of this building up and it will take time to heal and get over this. He is right, again. God gives us time to reflect and learn when we take the time. He knows everything. I have read my Bible and know His word is true and the verses that tell me not to be anxious, *"casting all your anxieties on Him, because He cares for you". (1 Peter 5:7) "When I am afraid, I put my trust in you" (Psalm 56:3).* There are many more verses to help but these two I use frequently. I can tell you and you can agree that it is easier said than done. If it was easy to follow Him, then we would have many more brothers and sisters in Christ. I did and still do place verses around the house to help me. Go grab some post it notes and get busy! Surround yourself with God's truth. We all need God's word. There is a difference in reading them, believing in them, and following them. Reading them…check. Believing them…check. Following them…still a work in progress. I do not keep the anxiety on purpose but it is hard to shake. Remember four years and counting to learn how to deal with anxiety and panic attacks. That is a long time to be miserable, sick, and enervated.

I want to release it and give it to Jesus because He already paid the price on the cross at Calvary. He paid it for me, you, and everyone else. If you have not accepted Jesus as your savior it is not too late, ask Him into your heart now, yes right now. We are all sinners and Jesus came to earth to bear our sins and offer us grace. Ask forgiveness of your sins and accept Him in your heart. *"For all have sinned and fall short of the glory of God, and are justified by his grace as a gift, through the redemption that is in Christ Jesus"* (Romans 3:23–25). God wants you as you are. I want to be done struggling with this. *"I have said these things to you, that in me you may have peace. In the world you will have tribulation. But take heart, I have overcome the world"* (John 16:33). God will keep me even when I am broken, when I am weak. I need Him. I do not have to be the strength,

God is. Why continue to live this way? God's word clearly states I don't have to.

Our family is involved in many events and ministries in our church. We should all be growing the kingdom of God somehow and kid ministry is something God has blessed me with. I love the littles. We love church. It's great to be in the building on Sundays but I also mean a church family, sisters and brothers in Christ. We make up the church, not the building. If you do not have a home church, reach out. Fellowship is important to growing in God. Even when we feel anxious and depressed it is essential to get out and be blessed by others in Christ. Being surrounded by your brothers and sisters can be one of the best gifts when we are struggling. No matter what the scenario is. Do not get me wrong I miss church sometimes because of my anxiety but I am able to watch the live stream! I am grateful for that. It is not easy to get up, get dressed, put on a happy face, and go out in public when we are fighting anxiety and panic attacks.

One Sunday, I tried doing just that, putting that happy face on while fighting the anxiousness. My happy face must not have been working because a few people asked me if I was okay, clearly, they could tell I was not myself and I think they were surprised when I said I was not good. They said they hope I feel better and I left it at that with a thank you and a smile. I sat down and sang during worship. I knew if I stood up, I would feel unsteady. As always, our lead pastor had an amazing message. Pushing through is hard, but I did it. You can do it as well. That is a victory in my book, and I haven't felt many of those these last few years. You will find your support in Jesus and He will send others to help at just the right time.

Chapter 8

DIG DEEPER

I have read many books and have studied through workbooks on this illness, disorder, sickness, whatever you want to call it and I felt none were of much help. None of the books I read said to *stop* and spend more time with our Lord. They gave techniques and verses, but I don't recall any telling me to be silent and listen for God during this struggle. The key is slowing down and finding rest in Him. Now, there are a ton of books out there on anxiety, I obviously did not read all of them. I wanted this to be a quick fix. I wanted God to show me what I needed to read or do to be healed. God wanted more from me.

I needed to just learn how to spend more intimate time with Him at this point. Quiet time with Him. Meditate on His words and truths. The Bible is our guidebook to learn and live from. We must stop, listen, and breathe slowly. I cannot keep running, do all the talking, and breathe fast and deep all the time. We know it does not work. Life is miserable this way.

Our battles are not as hard to deal with when we completely allow Jesus into our lives. If I want to see better days and stop holding myself hostage and pleasing Satan, then I give it to God. I know you have heard family or even friends tell you to just get over it and it is all in our head. Like we have not tried that a million times! This makes it harder for us to talk about our problems. This is one of the many reasons I became an introvert when I have always been an extrovert. Honestly, they cannot even come close to knowing what it feels like to live with these symptoms every day. Our brains won't even shut off to sleep! Our minds can have a million things going on. Being afraid, worried, anxious, depressed, and having panic attacks are paralyzing. But…there can be different tactics to try to help us. I know you have heard these lines before.

Look for triggers that you know make you anxious. For me I have noticed that dealing with our finances stresses me out, so now my husband does all the finances and that has helped. I still think about it, but I try to push it out of my head when the thoughts of not having enough come to mind.

If I have a long list to get done and start to feel chest pains or breathe heavy, then I stop looking at my list and go play with our son. If I am feeling anxious about leaving the house and driving somewhere, guess what, I do not leave the house that day. It is okay to slow down; Jesus was never in a hurry. Some people like breathing exercises and journaling. I love Bible journaling. Sometimes these can help me calm down enough to get through the rest of the day, other times it just does not work. Most of the time my body is just worked up and I have no idea why.

Maybe you do not have someone to relate to, so here you are, know that I am praying for you, you are not alone. I'm suffering with you, but *God is with us*! We are human. Anxiety can look different for all of us struggling. Sometimes God allows these difficult times to test us, step out in complete faith, to walk on water with Him and not look down. (See Matthew 14:26–34.) I unfortunately have looked down many times. I feel like I am drowning with a heavy rock attached to my foot but at the same time I have a life vest on. Just imagine how uncomfortable that is! That is because of Satan. Keep your eyes on Jesus. Look up when Satan says look down. Feel God's strength in you! The Holy Spirit will carry us.

Anxiety is an internal battle and it is serious. This is where Satan finds delight and he deserves no joy from our suffering. None! I will fight and win because God says I will. We serve a big God. You can do this! I have not given up and I will not. Now that is my competitive side. We can be our own worst enemy sometimes. For me it is most of the time and I must get this under control. I want to be a faithful servant, but Satan tries to invade and attack my faith. The war on my soul and yours is real. I pray you are strengthened by God's word and use it daily. I know what it feels like to want to give up. Multiple times. Lift your eyes to heaven. Jesus fought and died for you (us)! *"For you were bought with a price. So glorify God in your body"* (1 Corinthians 6:20).

We are surprisingly good at hiding our feelings so smiling is what we do on the outside. Let us feel good on the inside! I am sure there are many more avenues I will have to take and bridges to cross and rocks to jump over but I can do it through God, and so can you. One puzzle piece at a time. The path we walk with God is never straight. Remember you are not alone, get on your knees and cry out. Search our Abba (Father).

My faith has been strengthened through this period. I know now why I have walked this path. I continue to press on and I know that puts a smile on God's face. I am his daughter! Just as parents are sad when kids do not listen and sometimes, they must learn from their own mistakes. It is the same with God. He is waiting for me, for you. Total surrender. As followers of Christ, we fall. He is there to catch us every time! I did not agree with that before because I had to be a strong Christian, my faith looked weak if I was not, right? *No way!* We were made to need God. It is a wonderful thing to feel wanted. Wanted by someone whose love is immeasurable, a love that is unconditional, a love that is forever. If you still have not accepted Christ as your savior, you're missing out on life, eternal life, fulfillment, true love, true peace. He wants you to be blessed, to feel His love, and share it with others even when we have anxiety. The best thing that can ever happen in your life is to be saved by the grace of God. To bow your head and pray for forgiveness of your sins and accept Jesus in your heart. He accepts you no matter your past. God loves you and He sent His Son to die for you. I cannot say it enough that He really truly deeply undoubtedly loves *you*! Seek Him and He will show you the way. He will fight your battles.

Chapter 9

RESIST AND PRAY

I have been giving Satan too much attention and credit. Not on purpose but I was so busy and consumed praying about my problems that there was no way God could break through to me because I was the only one speaking. I once said to my husband it feels like God turned his back on me because nothing is changing. I have tried so many things. I have prayed so many times. My husband said, "No, we turn our backs to Him." Immediately I was mind blown. My husband's right, again. My husband is exceptionally good at being right. I agreed. My back was facing God without my knowing I was doing it. Again, because my situation was not changing, it did not mean God was not there and with me. Be prepared to fight Satan anytime you seek God. In James 4:7, we are told to "submit yourselves," then to God. Resist the devil and he will flee from you. Do not try to battle without God, we know where we have ended up before. We do not win, ever. We must gain control of our thoughts and for someone that struggles with a mental disorder that is just not easily done. Our thoughts and words are powerful. My thoughts throw my body into panic attacks. *"Be alert and sober mind. Your enemy the devil prowls around like a roaring lion looking for someone to devour. Resist him, standing firm in faith, because you know that the family of believers throughout the world is undergoing the same kind of sufferings"* (1 Peter 5:8–9). Never underestimate the power of Satan! *"In their case the god of this world has blinded the minds of the unbelievers, to keep them from seeing the light of the gospel of the glory of Christ, who is the image of God"* (2 Corinthians 4:4). Satan will stop at nothing to keep us held captive and in chains. He will try every trick in the book no matter the cost. He is not playing around.

Satan has crippled me for so long and I am done. Are you? Let us fight this with truth. God's truth! *"As for you, you meant evil against me, but God meant it for good"* (Genesis 50:20). God fights in my corner. I will not allow Satan to continue winning this battle and using me as a playing piece in his game. Satan is quiet when we stay idle or do what we want. There is no need for his intervention if we are not trying to grow God's kingdom, or strengthen our relationship with God, or seek God's help. *"The thief comes only to steal, and kill, and destroy" (John 10:10).* Even as I sit here and struggle with anxiety related pains I will push through because I feel God calling me to this journey and Satan wants me to give in and give up. Resist the devil (Matthew 4:1–11)!

As I reflect on my prayer life over the past few years, I only prayed for physical and mental healing. I should have been praying for wisdom and guidance to beat this. I cannot give it all to Him and in the same breath hold on to it. We live and learn right? I know God has heard every one of my prayers and I feel He was just trying to tell me, "Mandi, I am here, I love you, calm down, *be still, and know that I am God' (Psalm 46:10)."* I was not listening in those times because I allowed my circumstance to be bigger than God. What are you allowing to be bigger than our creator? Instead of praying over the bondage, pray for freedom. When I argue with myself and realize it, I start to repeat verses and focus on the positive. This can be so hard when our bodies are physically doing things that we can't seem to stop no matter how hard we try. We are fighting ourselves. This is the hardest thing I have ever dealt with.

Continually be in prayer with God. The time is now! When you first wake up praise Him, thank Him, and ask Him to help you in the areas you struggle with daily. He will! Use scriptures. Before you eat, pray for your meals, praise Him more, thank Him, and if you are struggling still ask Him to help. It is important to express ourselves. Lift a prayer for strength and guidance. Sometimes I have a good day after I wake up but by lunch, I am exhausted and need to regain strength in His word and need to pray. Before you turn in for the night praise Him and thank Him for the day.

There is no right or wrong way to pray when you pray from your heart. Being quiet and listening to God takes time. I am still learning. It is not an option to just go to Him quickly and be done. You will not get anywhere. We were created to be in a relationship with Him. Relationships take time. Now there is nothing wrong with sending God some short prayers, but it is important to spend quiet uninterrupted time with Him. This is how we grow. This is where we feel His presence. This is what will help us through the days we feel like we are not going to make it. Remember we need to use His word. God did not give us the Bible just to skim through it or collect dust on the shelf. It is our study guide to be close to Him.

It has been a hardship, but I can still smile knowing there is a day I will put this all past me. I took the stress and let it grow until I could not handle it anymore and this is where it got me. I am not saying that for you, we all have different circumstances and there are different types of anxieties. Turn to our Father in heaven.

Jesus came to die and suffer for us; we are not worthy of that. He chose to take the big one for the team—the *whole* team. He wants what is best for all of us. He wanted us to have an opportunity at eternal happiness. Amen! I should be filling my prayer time with being still and listening. I cannot allow Satan to come in and steal my prayer life. You do not get far when he stomps in and whispers lies. Praise God only, and often!

Chapter 10

LECTIO DIVINA

I attended a Sunday school class that was led by our family life pastor. The first part of the lesson asked why we study the Bible. Many of us gave our answers and to all our surprise not one of us mentioned that we did it to know God. We had great answers like how to treat each other, how to parent, have more knowledge of the Bible, friendships, personal growth, etc. but we missed the mark big time. The next question was how do study the Bible. We attend church, small group studies, devotionals, Bible journal, listening to Christian music, and radio sermons, which are great ways to study the Bible. Then our pastor mentioned a head study versus a heart study. I felt at that moment the Holy Spirit led me to this class. I was excited to learn about the heart study. What exactly did that mean?

A head study is when we learn the Bible through devotions, Bible study groups, inductive study, and CRU technique, to name a few. He used the inductive study as an example that moves from specific to general. It applies three principles to the text. First observing, what does it say? Next interpreting, what does it mean? Lastly, applying it. What does it mean to me? This technique is great for a head study. I realized I have been good at learning the word, remembering verses, and have knowledge when in conversations with others about the Bible. I can remember stories of the Bible and share them with our son and others. I like to watch Bible history and documentaries. Knowledge is there but I was missing something. That something is what I have been praying for, to feel God's closeness with my anxiety.

Our pastor then taught us about the heart study. So, the heart study is called Lectio Divina. This is Latin for Divine Reading. This is a great way to study the living word privately. There are four steps. The first is Lectio and that means to read the word. You will just take a small passage from the Bible and read it. Do not try to take more than eight to nine verses. At that moment I acknowledged I read the Bible by books and chapters and bit off more than I could chew. First, just read the passage and ask yourself what is this about? Forget for a second what you may know and just simply read the text. What stands out about this phrase or scripture? The next step is Meditatio and this means how is my life touched? What verse is sticking out to me? What is God calling my attention to? The third step is Oratio meaning is there an invitation? Am I invited to do something with this? What is God saying to me? And then, Contemplatio meaning to rest in prayer. Take time to pray over the verse or phrase that God is speaking to you. What does He want you to do with it?

After learning these steps, our Pastor asked us to individually look up the same verse and try this heart method. I thought it would be a lot harder to do but I read the passage and went through the steps. I was underlining and writing out each step and what I felt God saying to me and the passage we covered was Isaiah 30:15–21. The second sentence in verse 15 says, "in quietness and trust is your strength." I was like *wow*! Thank you, God, for answering my prayer. God knew I needed this lesson and put me there on purpose! Everything made complete sense then. I was trying so hard and doing so much but it was the head study I was acing, not the heart study. I did not know the difference and now God has equipped me. I plan on doing a lot more heart studies now that I understand how to do them. I invite you to learn this divine reading. It will draw you closer to God and bring peace during your trials.

Chapter 11

CONTROL

Another Sunday rolled around, and I did not want to go to church. I had to go because I was overseeing the welcome table, where you greet people with a happy face, answer any questions, hand out some information, and guide them if need be. I was not feeling it that day but I still went. Now do not get me wrong I love seeing and talking with people just not when I am having an anxious day. Unfortunately, I have many of those days. Our family life pastor had a message and let me tell you, God wrecked me that day! It has been years of dealing with anxiety and panic the way "I" wanted to, but every word that flowed from our pastor's mouth hit me deep, real deep. I did not think I would make it through the entire message. The Holy Spirit was working me over. He was talking about control and pride. Man, I was a mess. Crying silently, tears flowing the whole hour! God knew I would be there. God revealed to me at that moment that I must give Him *total control* to find true peace, to find relief. What do you need to give over to Him?

When we got home, I immediately sent our pastor a text message asking him to meet with me about his message. I was thankful he penciled me in that quickly and I met with him the next day to fill him in on what I felt during his message and he gave me some guidance. He invited me and my husband to a new small group he was starting. This is not a study that will last a few weeks or a few months. This study is meant for long term and building relation-ships with others and how to find rest in the chaos. Perfect timing again from God! Another answered prayer. We each have an accountability partner and check in weekly and attend a class during Sunday school. We have been in the group now for a while and it has helped me to find the calm in the storm. To know that there are things that can wait, and I find more joy in my life even though I still suffer with anxiety. My days have been better, and I look forward to where the study will take me. Nothing God does is by accident. God knew I needed to give up the control, God knew I needed rest, God knew I needed this study, He knows all!

I told my husband, "I am done fighting." Satan knows I am a fighter. This is where the MMA octagon would come in handy, but I do not have to put him down for the count, Jesus already did that. He fights our battles. It has finally clicked that no matter how I feel, what I do, or do not do, God is in control. The control did not start when my anxiety did. Being in control has kept me from God's peace my whole life. I keep the control when I refuse to feel anything less than strong. I feel so much time has been lost because of control in my life. I can pray that my future holds blessings and an end to a life sentence of fear, worry, anxiety, panic, and control. Jesus came to save the world. To save me, you. I want to get to a point where I feel normal, a day when my anxiety does not suck the life out of me. Satan has been happy to hold me captive for years. I need to remind myself multiple times a day, Jesus came for me. This is not the life he set before me, or you. I need to be willing to do whatever it takes to be free. Not what I want to do but what God wants me to do! Yes, God, not me, not you.

I have tried everything else my way, but I must be faithful and trust Him wholeheartedly. I am real, I am human. Getting to a point where I take medicine again is stepping out in faith and giving up control. I have fought too long and too hard to still be paddling in a circle and it is time to give it all up and through prayer and faith know He has me under His wing. *"He will cover you with His pinions, and under his wings you will find refuge; his faithfulness is a shield and buckler"* (Psalm 91:4). Time for control to be a thing of the past. What does your future hold? Do not allow Satan to keep dragging you down. Remember I know how you feel and if I can make it through this, you can too! There is power in the name of Jesus. Where is He? With you.

Chapter 12

CURRENTLY

I have had three panic attacks in the last few months. I know I had some added stress and it is just what happens. The bad thing is one of my attacks lasted for over two hours. Unfortunately, I'm not a person who gets a panic attack and it's gone in a few minutes. I was shaking, having trouble breathing, exhausted, and you know that list can go on forever with symptoms. I have always carried medicine with me just in case I have to take it, but I have had a strong fear of all medicine since the start of all this. Nonetheless I have carried it with me for four years and keep it close. So, I held a pill and prayed; my best friend was with me and helped me get through it but I didn't take the medicine. I prayed a lot that night.

The next morning, I felt different. I was more at peace trusting God that I took a pill that morning and had a manageable day. I told God it is His way now, not my own. No take backs! A few days after that attack I had another one driving home from my best friend's, that was scary. It is a three-hour drive and my husband was headed back from a mission trip in Jamaica. I again thought I would die or pass out and our son was in the back seat. I prayed, took the medicine, and called my biological father. He talked with me on the phone until I reached him and eventually made it home. Read this next sentence slowly. My pastor's message of control was just before I took this trip to see my best friend, the timing is all God. So, what does my future hold? Where do I go from here with the anxiety? Why do I still have the thorn in my side like Paul experienced:

> *So to keep me from becoming conceited because of the surpassing greatness of the revelations, a thorn was given me in the flesh, a messenger of Satan to harass me, to keep me from becoming conceited. Three times I pleaded with the Lord about this, that it should leave me. But He said to me, "My grace is sufficient for you, for my*

power is made perfect in weakness.
(2 Corinthians 12:7–9a)

I believe if this were not happening in my life that I would not have recognized my control and pride. I need to shake it off my sandals and leave it. God is in control; *He* is in control. We can find joy when we trust in the Lord. Life will be better when I give it all to Him.

I have also seen my doctor and I am taking medicine each day and we have talked about a plan. Although I had a bad reaction and side effects to the other medicines, I feel God telling me that this is the way we need to deal with this…for now. I have noticed I do not need to take deep breaths as often and I am sleeping a little better. Every day is different, and I know this medication is just temporary and my doctor wants me on something different, but this is a start. I'm leaving it up to God and what He sees fit and He has control. I must believe and have complete faith. I will be seeing a new therapist right at my doctor's office which is perfect because the office is only two minutes from me and they have evening hours. She is a Christian and I am going to stick with it this time and see where God leads me. Even if I have to write down all my worries. I must follow even if I am not comfortable. Anxiety is not comfortable. No worries about a babysitter, my son and husband can have guy time. Letting God lead me and be in with both feet.

The last six weeks have been very trying because we are currently stuck at home with the Covid-19 chaos and we do not know when it will end. The first few weeks of the stay at home order I was doing okay but as time goes on, I am feeling more depressed and anxious and now my doctor wants to increase my medication. I have only left the house a few times to ride in the car with my family for a little bit. The weather has been cold and rainy. I have wanted to stay in bed and my appetite has decreased more. Although presently I am more of an introvert, I feel claustrophobic being at home twenty-four seven. I've tried to take this time and enjoy the quietness of life, but it has been hard at times. I was thankful my husband was able to be home the majority of the time in the last month and I really needed him. I kept my mind busy with DIY projects and I love spending time with my husband. Our son is struggling more as time goes on. We have not been anywhere or seen anybody, even his grandparents. We are doing our best social distancing and adhering to the guidelines. This has been a great opportunity to teach our son that God is in control and He knows what we need and we have to find the blessings and that's not hard to do at all when we take the time to rest and be aware of what He created for us. We take God for granted sometimes and keep him in a small box. Our God is so much bigger than that and He has done everything for us. Take time to write down all the positive things in your life each day. I bet you will have a notebook full of goodness too!

I really wish I could end this book with… I am anxiety-free, but reality is will I ever be? Only God knows. I can do this with God and do it the way God wants me to do. I have run out of steam. Will I at least be able to control it so I can live life outside of my home, drive and shop by myself without my husband, enjoy my family without worry, do things I've held back from doing because of my anxiety? I pray one day I will. I need to focus on the now. We will have bad days but the good days and knowing where we are in Jesus conquers all. Let us conquer the demon and live the blessed life. As our Lead Pastor PD once said in a sermon, "My peace is not found in my health. My peace is found in my God." God bless, my friend.

REFERENCES

Anxiety and Depression Association of America (2010–2018). Retrieved from https://adaa.org/about-adaa/press-room/facts-statistics.

ABOUT THE AUTHOR

Mandi lives in Pennsylvania with her husband of eleven years and their eight-year-old son. She is a stay-at-home mom and homeschools their son. She enjoys the outdoors, geocaching, and metal detecting. She likes to crochet and loves crafts of all kinds. You can find her creating projects with paper, vinyl, wood, and even tools from the garage. If there is a garden or greenhouse nearby, you will find her there. She helps her local library with the community garden. She is involved in her church and has a heart for those in need. She felt God calling her to write about her journey with anxiety and panic attacks and how her faith is helping her get through each day.

Lightning Source UK Ltd.
Milton Keynes UK
UKHW011141171221
395825UK00001B/61